Mithlia

Mithlia

Mari Jamal

Dedicated to M and J,
your support has meant
so much over the years
I don't know what I
would do without both of
you.

Mithlia

Mari Jamal

Halbaffe Press

Minneapolis, Minnesota

© Copyright 2023 Mari Jamal

All rights reserved. No reproduction, copy, or transmission of this publication may be made without written permission.

No part of this book may be reproduced or transmitted in any form or by any means, electronic or mechanical, including photocopying, recording, or by any information storage and retrieval system, without permission in writing from the publisher. Please refer all pertinent questions to the publisher.

Any person who does any unauthorized act in relation to this publication may be liable to criminal prosecution and civil claims for damages.

The author has asserted her right to be identified as the author of this work in accordance with the Copyright, Designs and Patents Act 1988.

First published 2023 by
HALBAFFE PRESS

Halbaffe Press in the US is an imprint of Sinensis Publications, a division of Sinensis LLC, registered in the USA.

Sinensis LLC
PO Box 24542
Minneapolis, MN 55424

ISBN-13: 9780578718385

Contents

Forward	i
Preface	ii
blush	1
flirt	18

Forward

Mari Jamal is a bright new poet, and we are grateful to be in her presence. She has a bold tone, and is a delight to read. Mari is anticipated to be one of the leading poets of her generation. She is a refreshing voice, and redefines what poetry is, what it means, to Arab-Americans and poetry itself.

S. Jones
March 2023

Preface

  This is my first book, so I am a little nervous writing this. I am better at writing poetry than I am at writing forwards, but here we are.
  Sometimes I am inspired by pure fiction, sometimes from past relationships.
Either way, it's a treat for me as the poet to delve into new situations and feel it out, as if seeing things from different angles, like a photographer.
  Hope you have as much fun reading this as it was writing it.
  I am thankful to all my readers. I still can't believe that folks are actually reading my poetry and it resonates with them.

     love,
     Mari Jamal

blush.

3230000

Maybe Zazoo
or Zazu,
like a cartoon
character?

But is it possible
to name
a human
or a vehicle
just numerals?

Maybe a cat

Pablo
or Henrietta?

How about just
Zazoooo
First, middle
four O's

or *three mil*
for short

pupperoni

Small person,
shattered conscious
raised by a psychopath
and a loving mother
nature versus nature
we sort out
the aftermath

why does he
not intervene enough?
still sorting out
their mistakes

our lives are
in our control.

i dated a ufo

well, an alien,
but not like,
an "illegal"
human.

just a bona fide
weirdo.

the kind
ladies warn
each other about,
and I never
listen.

it didn't benefit me
but then
what did?

frivolous romance.

trophy husband.
someone who could
afford to look for love.
the rest of us
had to pay our bills
get a decent education
keep checking off
mom's vicarious
bucket list

happiness
was what mysteriously
happened
to other people.

you asked me
what I wanted,
I said let's start
with a budget
you asked me again
but didn't correct me.

how did I know
there was more

to life?
undone.

no regerts.

remember when
we were younger
and a force to be
reckoned with?

what happened
to us?
maybe bitter bitches
tried to break us,
but we're still
the same.

pint-sized nutcase.

I wish you well
in life
as long as you
stay away
from me
and my loved ones.

jealous toxic bitter bitch,
find a remote
tropical island
on the ends of the earth
and stay there.

I couldn't care less
if you win the lottery,
or meet someone nice,
just don't come back.

endlessness.

if you love me,
you had to cherish me,
not introduce me
to your
garbage friends.

you had to assess
your true priorities

you had to not
take me for granted.

I used to have
nightmares
about your friends.

you are so oblivious
that they are dealers,
and freaks.

ditch them
or leave me.

July 8th.

the strong wind
made the water choppy
but i saw G
swimming towards
the 'cool kids' dock
near the middle,
and i got jealous,
this would be
another thing
to cross off
my bucket list

im an okay swimmer, right?

but the weight
of my womb
dragged me down
and I couldn't float
on my back,
(my "emergency" move!)
the big waves waters
entered my lungs
i going to die,

oh Bahá'u'lláh!

I called out to G
a former lifeguard,
he grabbed me,

puzzled
why was I
in deeper water,
and dragged me
 to the shore.

i sat on the beach
in shock

definition of a bastard.

what kind of
monster
has kids
only to subject them
to helplessly
watching your
hedonistic lifestyle
from a corner?

you hid his toys
in the basement,
because children's things
interfered with your lifestyle?

who fills a fridge
with only booze
and no milk or water?

you are the excessive one,
you are the one no one wanted.

odyssey.

why
did we have
to sit here,
miles apart
years on end
as if we had no choice?

you chose this,
you know
you chose this

I thought you
were better at
pursuing your heart
than me,

maybe I had
to remind you how.

say it

tell me
you love me
through physical
means
often

you treat me
with respect

but refuse
to validate
what is there,
energy
doesn't
lie

neither does
life.

love you

I love you
too much
to put
my big old
ego
between us

I want you
to be happy
and have
the best
things in life

so avoid me
until it gets better

I love you.

<u>brave</u>

scrawny
insecure
lil' 20 year old
beast

I didn't know
much,
but I knew
I was proud
of every
perfect imperfection,
idiots might gawk
but this was
the real Aphrodite

wish you
felt the same

we were gangly
all feet and hands
but as cast from clay,
this is the real beauty
if you could

flirt

<u>flirt.</u>

such a dork,
didn't even make
sense,

what's the point
of meeting
somebody's
great grandpa
if you can't
even play?

so early
in the morning
I didn't even
know what
sanctity was…

I didn't know
what *wild*
was before
I looked
in the mirror.

<u>sometimes we don't think</u>

sometimes
we do dumb stuff
but we move on,

don't usually
look back
until years
later, when
there is a
world wide
pandemic,
and we are stuck
alone with ourselves.

<u>on the topic of,</u>

this could be worse.

<u>facing oneself</u>

for some,
it's as agonizing
as therapy
when you are
your own
therapist.

talking to
an empty
chair,
ruminating
endlessly
on every embarrassment
every failing,
feeling self-conscious
and shitty.

who judges you
when no one
is there?

no cash.

sorry bud,
didn't mean
to put you
in an awkward
position

sometimes
I'm a thimble-brain

I didn't realize
you were actually
like me,

you reminded
me of my dad,
I thought
you were buying
for both of us.

left behind.

I don't know
what happened
but it made sense
at the time

afterthoughts,
and too much
lifelong
compassion,
or a desire
to stay away,

I felt alright,
it wasn't
the worst idea
until winter
came.

needed to think
it through.

mirage

they talk,
you see?

this is
their resting
place
where they
sometimes
hover,
or maybe
we are
closer
to love,
there?

<u>underworld.</u>

somber
sunshine

electric
sky

yearning
to meet

yet deeply
patient.

<u>emptiness</u>

pieces
of me
left behind

I don't
think I'll
ever make it
without
some outward
acknowledgement
of my loss.

y not?

you could
have kissed me

you could have
asked for
permission
first
but you didn't
have to

I always loved you,
even before I knew
it was you

I just thought you
were a weird creep
at one point,
but I'm glad
we got to know
each other
and have
an understanding.

eff

to manage adults
is a goal for
someone else…

I never wanted that.
but as they age,
I end up helping
with odd tasks,

sometimes questioning,
as i line up
the ducklings,
is it poor hearing,
or cognitive abilities?

maybe my
hypochondriac
senses extend to them?

so confused,
what is reality
or perception?

later

I look around
on the map,
there are meaningless
acronyms everywhere

a tiny box
of chocolate milk
made
to fatten
one up.

I hover,
halfway outside
the subway car
coursing
through the sky.
Someone pulls
me inside,
and I lay flat
kissing the floor,

don't remind me,
we're still
in midair.

hair.

shocking plume
fluorescent jaune
popping
tufts backlit
by the sun

double-take
thank God
you don't do that.

reeling.

electric currents
flash over my
tongue

I blink, laughing
involuntarily
as if I just got punched
but am still standing.

why such accusations,
who can think straight
when knocked down

am I supposed to defend
myself, is this a game

I don't know how to play

<u>hopes for.</u>

don't pray
that I turn out
like you.

constant threats
to one's safety
made you
who you are,

it's a different era.
we don't need it.

buttercup.

you don't
need me
the way
I need you.

I wish you
could get
a taste
of what I mean

life akimbo,
freefall,
is this real
am I suffering
or is there
another path?

I don't blame you

kids

we didn't know
half of what we did,

how could we?

so much of what
we distilled was
a mashup
of pop-culture
and our values
and half answered
questions

society is for the masses
we had to help them
and us.

demon.

Precious little boy

When you
text me
we're on the same
page,

then you
let your
demons out
and they consume
you too.

Abandoned child,
still searching
for mother

still fighting
for survival

Honey, you are safe now
no need to fight anymore

mithlia.

Sitting at a party
in someone's house,
and you came
with some friends.
We talked
for about 5 minutes
but I felt
I was boring you,
so I got up
and walked away

sincere regret!

I should have sat
and got your number!
But nerds like us
didn't think that far
back then.

<u>can you see my tears?</u>

how cute
do you think
I still look,
wrinkles, skin tags,
eczema
and stretch marks

i try
to showcase
a new feature
in each selfie
so there's no
surprises

i know you
are shallow
and scared

but this is it

and all you have.

k

the difference
between her and you…

you glanced at me
from your chair
that NYE

had i replaced you?

at the time
i hadn't realized
that we had
drifted apart…

in hindsight?
a thousand times yes!

in reality,
neither of you
are worth shit.

gariyay

"when it rains, I cry"

or at least that is
what i assume
the word meant,
a double entendre
sadness and rain

but I was wrong

People say
you can learn
a second
language
if you heard
it as a kid.

Not true.

Somethings
I can never
pick up

Like my mother's
delicate femininity,

or my father's
dull hoofed
path through life.

<u>no words.</u>

she interrogates me
how we met,
how i know
your friends,
where did i stay
etc.

I don't even
know
what to say

your friends
are crazy
bitches

we stayed
at your place
but only
part of the time
because i am
terrible
with directions

also, i lost
my phone

nobody understands that part.

rain

Rain is theoretically
a happy concept,
when you are inside.

however, when you
party outside

and you want
to make it rain
at the rave,

but not actually
rain-

<u>crushed chips.</u>

standing on the train at night,
amidst a musician
and dancing
commuters,
I think of
some guy, moving
from car to car

when fun was allotted
to the masses equally

when the populace
got together,
on the bus ride home,
and a musician
would play for everyone

or the theater
would practice
with their windows
open,
so anyone
in the street
could get a free concert

standing in the alley below,
you could feel
a glimpse of life

<u>summer nights.</u>

summer nights
on a repurposed
urban prairie

how many
times
did we
blame Kris?

we knew
it was us

gentle warm
breezes kiss
my bare skin
with potential

unfulfilled,
devoid
of promise,
this year.

love me

"ok, grandma"
said sarcastically,
to an actual
gma

not exactly
hiding
myself,
not stating
the obvious
either,
waiting anxiously
for the future,

not a textbook case,
aches and pains
that don't make sense,
nothing never not helping

conservative family,
you can't handle
my love,
can't handle me.

trumpet

she is such
a devout fool
I didn't think
she had any inkling
ambition in her
beyond praying
and pleasing
her bitty version
of Reality

winter

brilliant cardinals
and chubby sparrows eat,
squirrels fatten up,
and my heart swells
a personal commitment
to stewardship for
neighborhood wildlife,
rabid feral rodents and birds

it just feels right.

hmm?

I love you
to pieces
but it's okay
if you repay
the sentiment
and tell her
we're still friends

wait, you're not mad
at me, are you?

Milton Keynes UK
Ingram Content Group UK Ltd.
UKHW010857140324
439440UK00015B/553